T0193640

Friends and Angels

MARIA ELENA GARZA

Copyright © 2015 by Maria Elena Garza . 704492

ISBN: Softcover   978-1-5035-4013-2
           EBook   978-1-5035-4014-9

All rights reserved. No part of this book may be reproduced
or transmitted in any form or by any means, electronic or
mechanical, including photocopying, recording, or by any
information storage and retrieval system, without permission
in writing from the copyright owner.

Rev. date: 02/05/2015

To order additional copies of this book, contact:
Xlibris
1-888-795-4274
www.Xlibris.com
Orders@Xlibris.com

Friends and Angels

MARIA ELENA GARZA

Contents

Seven Women.. 2

The Purse 4

Reflections 5

A Letter to My Every Part..................................... 6

A Promise 7

Growing Old 8

Wrinkles and Gray Hair 9

Angel Wing 10

"Baby" 11

Cup of Life 12

Christmas Gift 13

Roses in my classroom... 14

Like an episode 15

Angel Footprints.. 16

A Birthday Gift for You, Santi 18

Seven Women

Once a month they meet
To share, laugh and eat
The men they leave at home
To fix the roof and paint the room
Where shall we meet they ask;
Is it here or is it there?
All arrive at different times
Some with messed up hair
traffic is a dare they say
They meet and hug and count
One is missing still; Is she coming? they all ask
Or is she stuck in traffic jam
Quickly catching-up on family news
Waiting for the missing one
they finally sit, hang their purses and their hats
table decorated with the gifts
while the waiter waits
They review the menu slowly
to their despair
can't have this
can't have that
oh what happened to our youth
just a toast please
they laugh and count again
Oh My Goodness we all are here
The missing one, was not missing
Oh My Goodness what happened to our youth
We can't eat, we lost count, we forget
But oh they laugh and plan the next month meet
They hope they don't forget
Whose birthday is it next month ?
Don't be late
Bring the tums

The Purse

Pink, purple, yellow or blue
Stripes or circles,
name brand purses
Crockadile purses
Which one will it be?
Big and large
Small and dainty
In the hand
Or on the shoulder
A friend to hold
A friend to have
secrets it will hold
The trips it's taken
To places told and untold
A comb, a brush always ready to perform
A lipstick red or pink with taste of cherries or bubblegum
A mirror who shows the fairest one of all
The purse is there… always quiet and a true friend
Don't leave without it; don't leave it behind

Reflections

You molded my body
And gave me a soul
From my past generations
you gave me a part

Deep within me
I carry some secrets
About
Distant places,
People I never knew and
Far way lands

...you took it all
Gave me a part....
And using your hands
You made me....

And I love you
What a perfect god you are

A Letter to My Every Part

I want you to know that I loved you
Before you came into this world
I thought about you and I loved you

Will you see the flowers that I now see
Will you listen to the birds sing?

And when you're quiet…..
Will you think about me?

Will you be able to see the world that I now see?

You are a part of me
And I lived a hundred or a thousand years ago
And I laughed and I cried and I lived…..
And I thought about you….
And I loved you
And I wondered if you would ever think about
Me!

A Promise

When we meet again
In another life

I will remember you
I will love you again

We will talk about this day
And reminisce

Or perhaps we will not remember much

Just know that we're together again
A hundred years have passed

Will you know my name

Growing Old

Growing old
Content with life
Believing
Living
Sharing

A new beginning
…..closer to the end?
Perhaps
A story has been told

The final chapter
Life was good
Life was sweet
Life was not mine to keep

Wrinkles and Gray Hair

Is that ME?

Look closer

Put on glasses

Looks like me

But it can't be

Looks like my mother

When did she get here?

Glad you came mom

I'm leaving now

Have a dinner date

Wow, you scarred me

For a bit

Thought that was me

On the mirror

But, that's YOU

Love you Mom

Come visit anytime

You look beautiful

With your wrinkles and gray hair

Is that me?

Angel Wing

I found an angel wing one day
It was laying on my bed
I picked it up
And knew
That soon she would be back

I placed it on a soft white pillow
And left a little note
It said…..
"I found your wing today,
You must have left it here;
I cannot stay and wait for you
I have a million things to do."

"Baby"

A few more days
To wait…
To know…
To be sure

My heart tells me you're there
You are a part of me
I've loved you every moment
I think about you
Can you listen to my thoughts?
Can you feel my love?

I will hold you
Oh so gently
I can see your smile,
Your eyes,
Your tiny fingers

You are a part of me
And, I've thought about you
I call you "my baby."
I am your grandma
You are a part of me

You are so loved
Can't wait to hold you
Can't wait to see you

Cup of Life

You see the woman
Sitting at the far end
Of this vastly empty room?

Her eyes are warm
They speak softly.

Her encounters have been many.
She saw you smile at your beloved
When he lovingly fed you with his fork

Her thoughts escaped her
To an eternity that past
Her eyes looked sad
Yet very kind
Her thoughts went back into her youth
When old she thought she never would

The days have turned to year
And life has passed her by…

I wish that I could tell her
Her beauty is unique
For she has tasted all the juices
The cup of life can give.

Her wrinkles are her witness
Of all that she's been through
Her hands are small and fragile
And they tremble as she speaks

Although I do not hear your voice
It must be
Faint and sweet
And you have had a taste of life
And I've had just a sip.

Christmas Gift

Dear Teacher,
I have a Christmas gift for you
My father made this….. for you
When I visited with him in jail on Sunday
He told me to thank you
for taking care of me
He wanted you to know that he wished he was with me this Christmas
He made this rosary for you
I like the pink, yellow and white yarn he used
I tell him all the things we do in your class
He thinks I am getting really smart
I tell him I feel happy
I'm not afraid when I am in your class
Thank you teacher
Merry Christmas

Roses in my classroom

I have a classroom full of roses
They all have special needs

I give them all great tender care
And watch them as they grow
While some grow nice and straight and tall
Some need my help before they fall

I quickly rush to help them up
For no one in my class will fall
They all must stand up straight and tall
And
I am there not far away
To help them grow
And
Stand up tall

Like an episode

life

Like an episode

The stage is alive
Unending

The world watches

The scenes change
Directing,
editing,
writing

a story has been told

Angel Footprints

Today,
I saw some footprints

They were crossing through my yard

I stood and saw the shape and size

And I quickly knew

An angel had been by.

He left his footprints
On the grass
So I would know that he had passed
On his way to far away
Where all the other angels
wait

A Birthday Gift for You, Santi

I could not find a thing to give you
For you have it all
You have many friends who show their love each day
You have the Lord in your life whom you pray to everyday
So.........
I gave it lots of thought
What gift could I give to a friend who has it all?
I asked the Lord for help
He is your son I said
Tell me what to do
And then I fell asleep
I woke up in the early morning hours when day had not arrived
I thought I heard a gentle whisper coming from above
I walked outdoors
And saw the beautiful stars shimmering with excitement
speaking volumes all at once
Oh!.............I said what a perfect gift
I give you your heavenly star
It shines the brightest among others; go outside this evening
And try to find your star
It will be the brightest looking down at you
Whispering ever so gently: Happy Birthday Santi sending you blessings from above

Printed in the United States
by Baker & Taylor Publisher Services